Shoebox

(A tiny little division of Hallmark)

You probably do some things differently now than you did 20 years ago. Well, so do we. We make fun of what is topical, and that changes, so the making-fun-of changes, too. There are things you wore in the mid-80s that you look at now and you're like, "that's so mid-80s." Same with jokes. Funny stays funny, but sometimes we look back at topics we made fun of once upon a while back and we're like, "Whoa!" We've learned, we've grown. A little.

Written by Dan Taylor & Shoebox staff writers
Edited by Jeff Morgan & Sarah Tobaben
Editorial Direction: Todd Hafer
Art Direction: Maura Cluthe & Kevin Swanson

Design: Mary Eakin & Christine Taylor
Flip-book Illustration: Renée Andriani
Handwriting: Mary Eakin
Production Art: Dan C. Horton
Cover Design: Maura Cluthe & Christine Taylor

Printed and bound in China

ISBN: 1-59530-118-6

First Edition, July 2006

10 9 8 7 6 5 4 3 2 1

Shoebox

GReatest Hits and Misses

Celebrating the 20th Anniversary
of America's Funniest Greeting Card Company

2000BOK6059

(A tiny little division of Hallmark)

Table of Contents

10. Pets Unleashed

22. Animal Instincts

32. Boys Will Be Boys

42. Girls Will Be Girls

56. Humor From A to DD

68. Butt Seriously Folks

80. Laughing Burns Calories

90. Humor Outlet

102. Only Teasing

116. Aging Disgracefully

130. It Only Hurts When I Laugh

142. Signs of the Times

152. A Hard Day's Laugh

162. Relatively Funny

172. I Do...What?

182. Adults Only Sextion

194. Controversially Speaking

200. Random Acts of Funny

216. Funny, But No

The History of Funny

300 Million BC — Dinosaurs roam the earth. Except for one, who trips.

347 AD — Some Roman Emperor named Chuck hears a joke and laughs just a little bit, thus inventing the "chuckle." Decades later, Chuck's son Chort will follow in his footsteps.

1582 — April Fool's Day invented. Just kidding! Or am I?

1876 — Alexander Graham Bell follows up his invention of the telephone with the stinging remark, "Hey, Watson—the 1860s called. They want their buckled shoes back."

70,000 BC — Neanderthal man discovers fire, prompting wiseguy friend Ug to become first ever to crack, "is it hot in here, or is it just me?"

953 AD — First bar opens. A guy walks into it.

1776 — Declaration of Independence signed.

Thomas Jefferson brings the house down by using the name "Jacques Strap."

Shoebox

(A tiny little division of Hallmark)

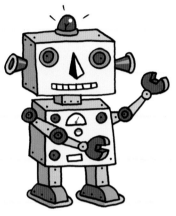

1920
Prohibition
outlaws alcohol.
There is nothing
funny about this.

1986
Shoebox Cards
are born. This
is the most
important thing
in the history
of the universe—
ever. Is too!

2000
Shoebox staff
replaced by robots.
No one notices
notices notices
notices notices
notices notices

1903
The Wright brothers
take flight. Upon
landing, Orville is
finally able to use
his well-rehearsed
line, "I just flew
in from Kitty Hawk
and man, are my
arms tired!"

1974
The Disco era is
in full swing
and, well, who
isn't laughing?

1993
The Global
Summit on E-mail
Abbreviations is
held. After hours
of heated debate,
it is decided that
"Laughing Out Loud"
should heretofore
be known as LOL.

2005
Some Shoebox
writer completely
makes up the
History of Funny.
So to you, we
say "Ha!"

click
click
click
click
click
click
click
click

ForeWord by
WiLLiaM ShaKespeaRE

A ROSE BY ANY OTHER... DRAT!! THese THiNGS ARE TiNY!!

Shakespeare's First Failed Career: Candy-Heart Writer

I've often wondered what I'd be writing if I were alive today. You hear people say "it's not exactly Shakespeare" whenever something's short and artless, which I guess is kind of a compliment, but were I to put plume to parchment today, what would come of it? Would I be writing greeting cards? Maybe so. They speak to the same kind of emotions and passions that my greatest works did.

Would I be writing Shoebox cards? No. First, they hardly ever use iambic pentameter. Second, they rarely mention Danish politics. Third, well, first and second were really deal breakers for me.

Obviously, I had a flair for comedy. You
don't name a character "Bottom" without chuckling.
And I did jokes about body parts, sure.
And I touched on parents driving you nuts,
kids letting you down, the everyday
frustrations that plague us from the halls
of the castle to the hovels of scullery maids.
Come to think of it, maybe I would write
Shoebox cards. How hard can it be? "Surely,
thou art no longer young!" Hey! Funny!
What'd that take me? A minute? I can drink
coffee and jerk around on the Internet
all day as well as the next bard. And
it's a whole lot easier than making everything
fit that stupid ABAB scheme, or whatever.

Yeah! I could be a great Shoebox writer.
If I weren't dead. It's always something.
Ah, well. Enjoy this book. It's not
exactly Shakespeare, but it's pretty good.

William Shakespeare

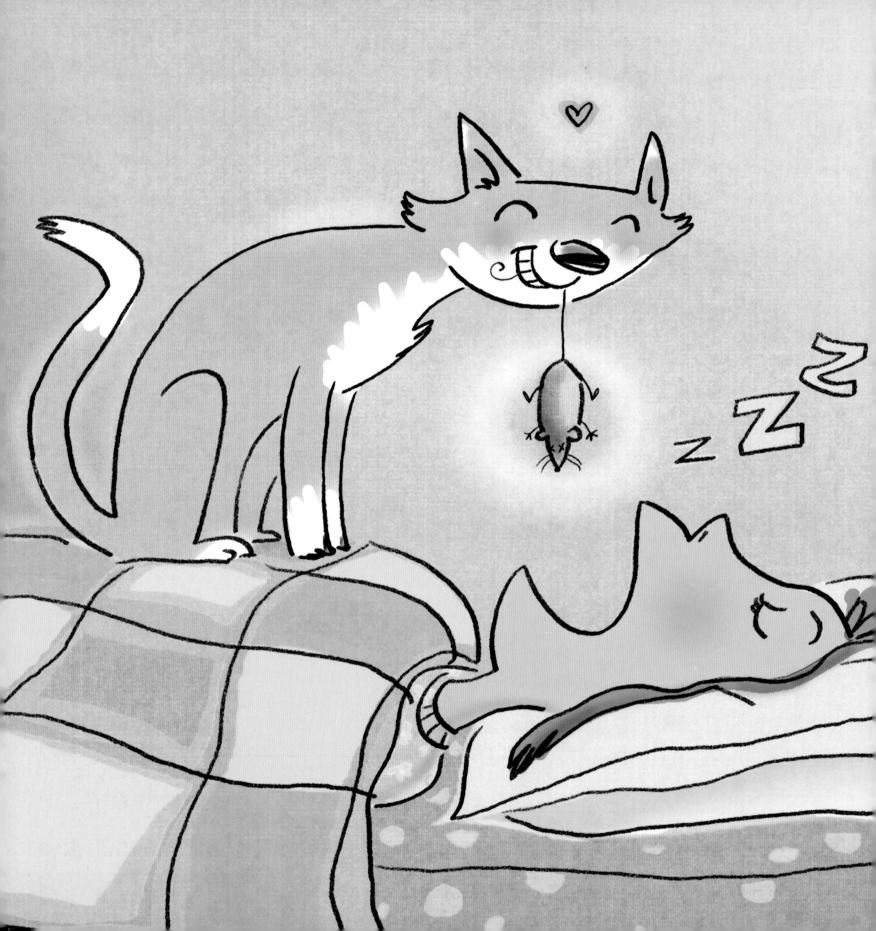

Pets Unleashed

Who makes a mess on the rug, tears
the leather couch cushion, and licks people
indiscriminately? Right. Your high school
boyfriend. But also cats and dogs.
And cats and dogs have an excuse. Dogs love
unconditionally. Cats, well, cats have strings
attached. But either way, we love them,
we care for them, we make cards about them.

Note: Most Shoebox staffers are
pet owners with dogs beating out cats
by a hair in popularity.

weird threat,
also overheard
in the lunchroom.

Dog romance

Awww, look what the cat
made for you today!

As gross
as this is,
ANYTHING
a dog could
form into
a heart shape
would only
be worse.

This card has
been in the line
a long, long time,
which may provide
some curious
insight into
our consumers.

If you ever thought too much about all the places in your home your pet has touched with his naked butt, you'd have to move.

Anita

inside:
Hope you find a nice place to eat your cake.

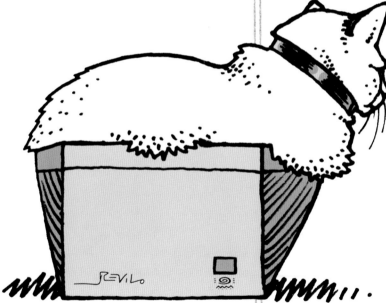

No cats were actually crammed into boxes in the making of this card. As a rule, we're ANTICRAMMISTS.

15-POUND CAT IN A SIZE 5½ SHOE BOX.

Dogs in human situations— Can't get enough of it!

inside:

DO:
Have a happy birthday.

DON'T:
Pee on your presents.

FIFI, A TRUE FRIEND, ALWAYS WARNED MARIE WHEN SHE HAD LINT ON HER BUTT FROM SCOOTING THE CARPET.

An Internet search for poodles was necessary for this drawing since no staff member owns one. we seem to favor <u>mutts</u>.

Written at a time when many of us were buying our first houses,

Rex buys a home.

Why golden retrievers don't make good tight ends.

How ironic, that the dog's name is Katowski!

CaTS oN dOGS

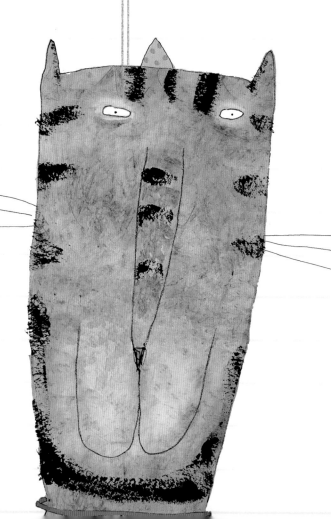

* Dogs are like scratching posts with sound effects.

* If they're so smart, why don't they know to keep their heads inside moving vehicles?

* Who cares who let them out?!

* Dogs are man's best friend. How sad for both of them.

* Just the ONE life? Losers.

* You can teach an old cat new tricks, so there.

* Anyone who's that happy to see you has got to be stupid.

Dogs on CATS

* Cats are pretty snobby for creatures who bathe with their tongues.

* "Tabby" rhymes with "Crabby." Coincidence?

* They think their litter doesn't smell. Well, um, it does.

* Often associated with witches. Just sayin'.

* Ooooh, a cat, I'm a burglar and I'm so afraid.

* Dog breath beats tuna breath <u>every</u> time.

* Give me a clue here... which end is the butt?

AniMaL INstincts

If you spoke even a little raccoon, you
wouldn't feel the slightest bit guilty about
making fun of animals. They joke about us all
the time. Right now a bear is doing an
unflattering impression of you getting into
last year's swimsuit. Deer are making
fun of the way you run. Do you think the birds
are picking cars at random?! Face facts.
And laugh right back.

If chickens
bought cards,
they'd be
OFFENDED.

Truly Wrong ⟹

Middle-Aged Chickens

Middle-Aged Chickens

Middle-Aged Chickens

Creativity, innovation, originality. These are three things you won't find here.

You will find three ways to do the same joke. Find the differences! (Hint: It's the artwork.)

I BOUGHT YOU A
STINKING HIPPO CARCASS
FOR YOUR BIRTHDAY.

And then I thought,
"Gee, a stinking hippo carcass
isn't a very good birthday gift."
So I'm keeping it in my kitchen
and giving you a card.

Might just
qualify as the
weirdest card
we've ever done.

inside:
You're getting
the better deal, believe me.
I almost wish
I'd never bought that
stinking hippo carcass.

I hope a BIRD doesn't PECK your eye out on your birthday, because then every birthday after that you'd say, "This is the ANNIVERSARY of the day a BIRD pecked my eye out."

Maria

inside:
Same thing goes for a WOLVERINE chewing your LEG off.

Written by Pegleg McSquints, who left Shoebox and became a pirate.

Perhaps the last-minute wolverine reference is a bit much.

If you're Happy
and you know it
CLAMP YOUR HAMS!

Only about ½
the people in
the department
got this. Must
NOT have gone
to summer camp.

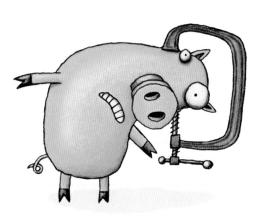

and a baa baa here, and a baa baa there

The writer of this card grew up on a farm, to the degree that joke writers ever grow up.

Old McDonald Has a Cow

31

Inter-species
mingling is
something Shoebox
neither supports
nor opposes.

BOYS will be BOYS

Boys grow into men, but they retain many
of the lovable traits they had when they were
eight. They also retain many of the goofy,
disgusting, and downright frightening traits
they had when they were eight. They may not
do that much growing after all. We'd feel kind
of bad about all the jokes we've done about
men, if not for one thing. They're just
so funny! See for yourself.

Note: An unknown Shoebox artist always
brings, and then leaves, the newspaper in
the bathroom. It is secretly appreciated.

Based on
an actual
3ʳᵈ
(and final)
date.

New Edible Underwear Designed by Men

The Six-Pack

The Nacho

Slurpees
and Beef Jerky

Please note:

These edible underwear designs **do not** fit in with a low-carb diet.

Led to a **BIG** discussion on why this couldn't work in real life.

October 7, 2005

Hallmark Cards
2501 McGee Street
KANSAS CITY, MO 64108

Attention: **Whoever is in Charge of Getting the Facts RIGHT!!**

Dear Sir/Madam

Enclosed is a photocopy of a Shoebox greeting card which I purchased specifically for my grandson who, at the age of 20, is currently on an extended tour of South America.

I learned about Lake Titicaca and its location in South America (the highest lake in the world) in the 1940's; Kyle (above-mentioned grandson) having actually been on Lake T. can also vouch for its location. However, someone in your firm really goofed when illustrating this card - as you can see, S. America is facing the front while the students are pointing somewhere close to the UK and the other children are looking at Asia!! They are all about as far away from Lake Titicaca as they can get!!

Better be more careful in the future!!

Sincerely

Jara

HOW A WOMAN SEES IT: HOW A MAN SEES IT:

Sea Spray → ← GREEN

Garden Moss → ← GREEN

Very Verde → ← GREEN

shoebox lore:
At least
10 million men
have a form of
color blindness.
Not so funny
now, is it?!

Card inspiration comes from many places, including the Victoria's Secret located near our offices.

Betty often wondered if it was too obvious her husband decorated the house.

Based on the apartment of a writer who's living room consisted of a large-screen TV and a recliner.

ON WOMEN

* Oh, no, go ahead. I wanted you to have most of my fries.

* Show me a man who understands women...no, really. I'd love to meet him and pick his brain.

* Everything you need to know about women: Be afraid. Be very afraid.

* Women are like poetry. I don't get poetry either.

* If not for women, we'd just spend all our time watching sports on TV and eating barbeque and...hey! Wait a minute....

On Men

✳ Whoever labeled women "the weaker sex" has obviously never tried carrying a purse.

✳ Men are good for one thing. Two, if they know how to make waffles.

✳ P.U.! What died in...oh, your friends are here to watch the game.

✳ Men are great. Just ask one.

✳ If men had to wear pantyhose, pretty soon nobody would have to wear pantyhose.

✳ "Women's Intuition" is just a polite way of saying, "Women are Smarter."

GiRLS WiLL be GiRLS

The average woman understands that there's no such thing as an average woman. Women communicate at a higher level than men can ever imagine or begin to understand. And that's just when they're talking about hair. Cards written for women are some of the best cards ever because, duh, they're written for the gender that buys most of the cards.

Note: Hard hitting, relevant, empathetic...written, you guessed it, by a guy.

Do you know how hard it is to get to work on time when some sexy hunk is urging you in a throaty whisper to come back to bed "for just one more minute"?

o'keefe

inside:

Me neither. Damn.

People _love_ this card. Not sure why.

Making fun of guys: Almost _too_ easy.

Jean and Alice were so glad they had
decided to check their husbands through
instead of carrying them on.

As you're recovering, just relax... Put your feet up... Have people bring you things... You know...

GORDON.

inside:

Pretend you're a man.

Also works with:

· Pretend you're a blonde.

· Pretend you're management.

· Pretend you're my kids.

Based on a
real birthday
celebration
in the
early 90s.

Tami's birthday was ruined when her
friends accidentally hired a _real_ fireman.

Jan read an article that said you should decorate with things you have lying around the house.

Why is the
dog sitting
at the table?
Extra humor,
that's why!

JUDY HAD A SPLIT
PERSONALITY. THE TOP HALF
WAS INTROVERT, THE
BOTTOM WAS NOT.

REVILO

53

Based on a very funny event that we can't talk about.

He loves me

He loves me *not*

He loves me

He loves me *not*

He loves me

(See Next Page)

WhAT's inSiDe?

(Choose Your Favorite Message)

✳ The "protein only" freaks mean
more cake for you!

✳ At least you're only getting gray hair
in places that already had hair.

✳ You'll probably get gift cards from
guys who don't know the first thing
about shopping!

✳ No ring on your finger, no slob
on your couch.   ⟵ The fourth option is the one that actually made it to print.

✳ You can re-heat your coffee
with hot flashes.

Where the Trouble Begins

HUMOR from A to DD

Boobs are a big target for humor.
Two big targets, actually. Or small
targets, which is also funny. You can't
do this many jokes shared between women
without getting to boob jokes. Some
of them are written by guys. Guys who are
very scared and very careful not to
make eye contact when the jokes get read.
Here's more than a pair of great ones.

Working staffers' names into the cards is always fun.

inside:

It only took one trip outside for Sarah to decide that the boob job was totally worth it.

inside:

Happy Birthday to a woman who hasn't given up hope!

Idea developed (NO PUN) after hearing about an 11-year-old who said something funny along these lines.

Madge thought the new "gravity-defying bra" went a bit too far.

Another bra joke written by a guy.

YOU COULDN'T FIND BETTER BOOBS THAN THESE? AND WHERE'D YOU GET THIS RIVER BARGE OF A BUTT?

ON

OFF

THE BRIDE OF FRANKENSTEIN LODGES HER COMPLAINTS.

 SPORT

 WORK

 CASUAL

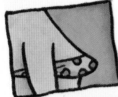 FORMAL

 PARTY

cleland

inside:

IF WOMEN COULD CHANGE
THEIR BOOBS AS EASILY
AS THEIR HAIRSTYLES.

RETIRED

shoebox lore:
In 1991, the
average bra
size in the U.S.
was 34B. Today
it's 36C.

The artist's request for A MODEL for this card concept was declined.

inside:
EVERY MAN'S BIRTHDAY FANTASY-- BEING BURIED ALIVE IN WARM CLEAVAGE.

S h __ __ b_ x

inside:
Your brains and your pride.
(What did you think I was
gonna say?)

The "Customers" in this card bear a striking resemblance to two of our artists. We've been told it's only a coincidence.

you have to
read a <u>lot</u>
of magazines
to find
beauty tips
like this.

A VALENTiNE'S DAY TiP:

TOO MUCH SHADING
TO CREATE CLEAVAGE
CAN BE MiSTAKEN
FOR CHEST HAIR.

Has been read on a reality TV show when it was a cast member's birthday.

This artwork came from a surprisingly thoughtful card that said,

"Hope you're holding up okay."

TOP TEN NICKNAMES for "Them"

10. Thing 1 and Thing 2

9. The Knocky Mountains

8. The Northern Delights

7. Cheese Nips (Wisconsin only)

6. The Pointer Sisters

5. The First Ladies of Hooterville

4. Sweater puppets

3. Lunch! (under toddler set only)

2. Knock, Knock, hey there!

1. The co-stars of "Leave It To Cleavage"

A list that will _never_ appear on a card... unless you tear out this page and make it into one, which we don't recommend.

BUTT SERIOUSLY, FOLKS

Butts are funny. You know it's true.
Think about butts for a minute and see
if you don't smirk. If your own butt doesn't
make you laugh, someone else's will. And
if your own butt doesn't make you laugh,
it might make you cry. So there you have it.
Butts cover the spectrum of human emotion.
How could we not do several, and by several,
we mean a lot, of cards about them.

This cartoon was based on a writer overhearing a woman on a subway in chicago say that a celebrity had <u>more</u> <u>cleavage</u> <u>in her boobs than</u> the woman did in <u>her butt.</u> It was immediately translated into a card.

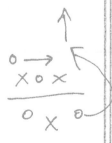

¡Pedro!

Unfortunately, when Madge wished for cleavage, she neglected to specify where.

if books had butts, they would look like this: ⟶

There have been two women named **LIZ** in Shoebox over the years. No comment beyond that.

we're still not exactly sure why butts crack people up.

inside:

Just wanted to send you a wisecrack on your 40th birthday.

Plumber Birthday Parties

Number 5... That's my boy!

Cosmetic Surgery for Plumbers

plumbers are the ~~butt~~ of many jokes.

Some jokes are so irresistible, we do them over and over.

This is based
on an actual
ongoing debate
between two
shoebox employees.
No one really wins
this kind of
debate.

It's your birthday.
My butt's bigger.

As long as you show a DONKEY, you can say whatever you want.

The old saying, "Unless you're the lead dog, the view never changes" reapplied to a Christmas card.

Christmas Eve, as seen by Santa

CLASSIC
butt humor
was what made
this country
great. Along
with cheese that
squirts out of
a can. Those
two things.

the other side of
Mount Rushmore

We use Cupid a lot at Valentine's Day even though no one is really comfortable with the armed baby idea.

...Tired of his thankless job, Cupid decides to shoot something besides arrows at would-be lovers.

BEGINNER GHOSTS

Without the candy, this illustration of a butt would not have fit the corporate guidelines— or last years jeans.

To resist eating Valentine's Day treats, Judy imagines all the little chocolates going straight to her butt.

Mitch decided he'd better start working out again.

Based on the fact that in 1985, the average waist size for men was 32. In 2003, it was 36.

Do you want fries with that stat?

Laughing Burns Calories

At any one time, 30% of the Shoebox
staff are on a diet. Another 30% are
planning a diet. 39% have just ended
a diet, and sworn to just give up and
never diet again. And 1% is the new girl
on the art staff who said she could just
"eat whatever she wanted and not gain
a pound!" She may have said something
after that, but she's dead
to us, so we can't hear her.

This idea came to the artist when his own dog had to wear the "CONE OF SHAME" during allergy season.

It's the latest thing. It's called the veterinarian diet.

I've found a great new diet-- the grapefruit diet.

inside:
You put a couple of grapefruits in your sweater and everything seems a lot more proportional.

GUESS WHAT?

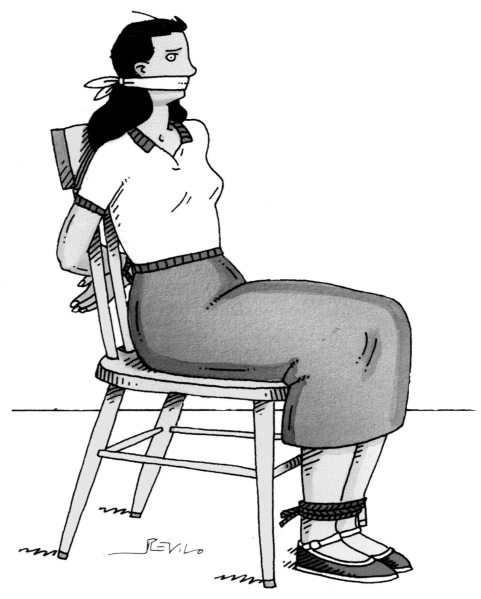

The artist of this card is said to base his drawings on real people. So if you see a guy with a sketchpad looking at you... run.

Chairs from the shoebox break room.

REVILO

inside:

I'VE FOUND THIS GREAT NEW DIET THAT REALLY WORKS!

SO WHAT'S NEW WITH YOU?

Whew! Just taking a break from polishing the silver and planning a week of gourmet meals to say hi before running to yoga class!

You don't want to know what "polishing the SILVER" is code for.

inside:

Right. And then I'm going to Jupiter, because I am their queen! Tomorrow, we invade the Planet of the Apes. Wish us luck!

Two classics...
People love
to hate
themselves.

I gotta buy some lighter underwear.

The SHoEbox Guide to WEiGht Loss

* To reach the ideal weight for your height, it's simple: Wear six-inch heels.

* Get your friends together on a regular basis and feed them gravy. Before you know it, you'll be the skinniest.

* If given a choice, go for the brownies with nuts, because nuts are low in carbs.

* Go live on the moon, where you only weigh 22 pounds. You'll be lonely, sure. But only 22 pounds of lonely.

* Look at photos of relatives.

* Try "the patch"—it goes right over your mouth.

* Lose weight fast...clean out your purse.

HumoR OUTLeT

"ONE SIZE FITS ALL" is maybe the most cruel
and mean-spirited phrase ever printed,
except when it comes to these cards. Because
shopping is something we take seriously. And
like everything that gets taken seriously,
that makes it a great target for jokes.
Jokes like these. Have a look, but remember,
if you break one, you bought it.

Note: Cartoon inspired by the disturbing
stat that 25% of all women's underwear
purchases are thongs.

Funny
because
it's true.

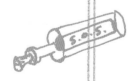

"Shop class" wasn't quite what Tina had expected.

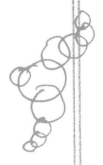

Author Bill Bryson has this to say about our national obsession with shopping—
"We used to build civilizations. Now we build shopping malls."

Written by a guy, as are many of the cards that appear to come from an insightful female perspective.

inside:

Clean living paid off,
and Leslie ended up going to Heaven.

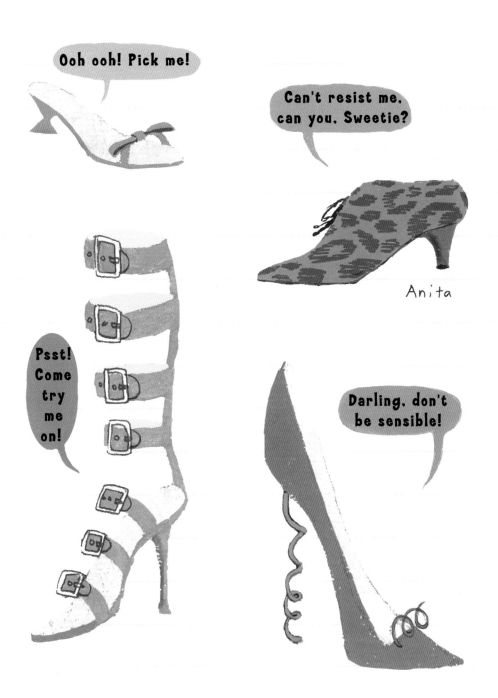

Anita

Voices Only Women Can Hear

People who say you can never have too many shoes have never had three.

This card was made into a poster that was displayed in Hallmark Gold Crown Stores nationwide. The artist didn't know until she stopped by her local store.

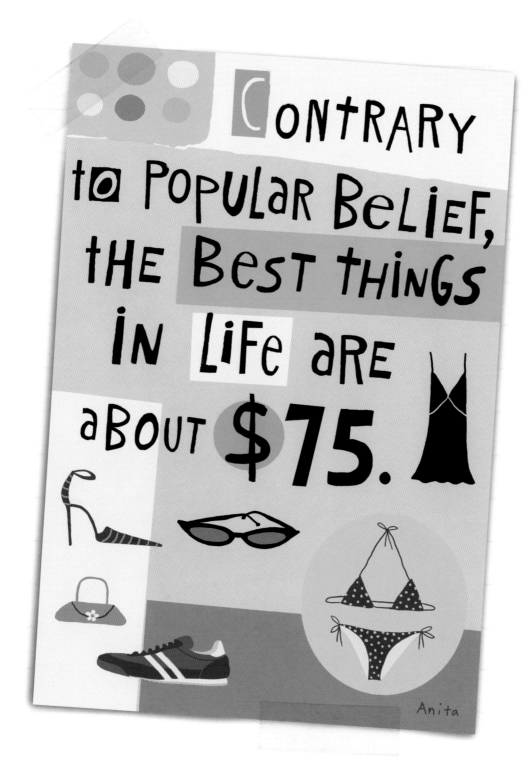

Or, if you believe the celebrity magazines, the best things are more like a gazillion _dollars._

"You can't have
too many shoes
or if you're
crazy, cats."

– Shoebox writer
and resident
shopping expert

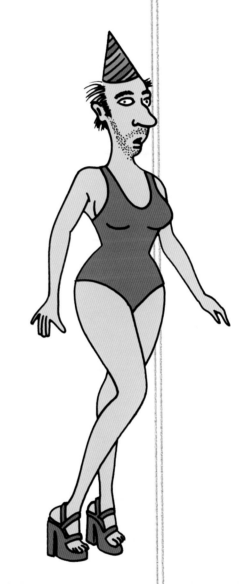

TIM SHOULD'VE BEEN MORE SPECIFIC WHILE WISHING FOR A BETTER BODY ON HIS BIRTHDAY.

SHOeboX FaShion & BEauty TiPs

* True beauty comes from within.
  Within a really expensive day spa.

* Smart women know that real beauty
  doesn't come from a drawer full of
  makeup. You need at least two drawers.

* "Natural" and "Beauty" go together like
  "Diet" and "Bearclaw."

* Cucumbers on your eyes are good, but
  olives in a martini are even better.

* Remember, if your Grandma wore it,
  it's retro. If your Mom wore it, well,
  your Mom wore it.

* Buy a pair of tight, low-rise jeans. And
  burn them. You won't look any different,
  but you sure will feel good.

* Surround yourself with ugly people.

oNLy TeasiNg

We are obsessed with hair. We wish we had
more in some places and less in others.
We want straight hair to be curly and curly
hair to be straight. We think it's funny when
someone loses his hair, and even funnier when
he finds it on his back. Just remember that
no one with so-called "perfect" hair is
really happy on the inside. Sure they may
look happy, but there's more to life than the
outside of the package. All the same, if you
could recommend a good conditioner....

Note: Her word balloon was re-written
like 7 times. The writer is still
not 100% happy with it.

Bob soon realized that his hair peninsula had broken off to form its own island.

Here we see the ever-present influence of one David Letterman.

Individual hairs are one of the hardest things for an artist to render.

inside:

40... it's not just a skirmish, it's war.

Inspired from waiting in the line a LONG time.

Baldness is comedy gold!

inside:

You've reached the age where shopping for hair products means going to the sunscreen aisle.

123 XyZ

卌

Hairy back.

Miss you.

This card was statistically proven to elicit the most "Ewwws!" from shoppers.

The rarely seen visual pun often doesn't get the humor credit it deserves.

The tip of
the blonde joke
ice-berg.

Surprise birthday parties
for blondes.

I don't believe it's true that blondes have more fun.

inside:

It's just that their attention span is so short, everything seems new and exciting.

"I have met the enemy and she is blonde with big boobs."

– Written by a brunette Shoebox writer

We bring our dogs
to work sometimes
Good for morale,
bad for carpet

I've had this same cut since
obedience school! Let's get crazy
with some layers! Oooh!
And highlights to bring out
my eyes! Then add some of
those darling little red bows
right over my ears!

Dave Loved His New
"Home Toupee Maker" Kit.
His Dog was Less Thrilled.

Merciful heavens! What hideous thing have you done to your hair? Shame on you! Now I must summon all my skills to correct this disaster!

Hair gets talked about more than politics, religion, and taxes.

COMBINED.

inside:

Avoid hostile makeovers on your birthday.

Do yourself a favor, <u>STOP</u> thinking about it.

inside:

GRAY HAIRS DON'T
HAPPEN JUST ON
YOUR HEAD.

A VALENTINE TRAGEDY--

NEVER even start thinking about it.

Inevitably Paris, the City of Love, became completely entangled in armpit hair.

REVILO

BOB GOT MORE THAN HE BARGAINED FOR WHEN HE WISHED FOR A FULL HEAD OF HAIR.

Top Ten Ways to Tell You've Got A Bad Haircut

10. As your hair is drying, your hairdresser is fired.

9. People suggest you become a firefighter just so you can wear a big hat.

8. Friends make sudden jerky movements to block your view of yourself in mirrors and windows.

7. Strangers involuntarily begin whistling
"Send in the Clowns" as you walk by.

6. You're constantly handed copies of
"From Lemons to Lemonade: A Guide to Coping."

5. Waiters ask if you'd mind eating
in the kitchen.

4. You notice mothers clamping their
hands over kids' mouths as you stroll
through the mall.

3. The slightest bit of humor makes people
burst into uncontrolled laughter, as if
they'd been holding it in for some reason.

2. A video of you just sitting around doing nothing
takes top prize on that funny video show.

1. You notice people doing that "I'm trying not
to look, but if I look away too quickly,
it'll be obvious I'm trying not to look, so
I'll try not to make a shocked face" look.

AGING DISGRACEFULLY

Some people say there is nothing we can do about aging. These people aren't in the greeting card business. Because the people who make cards say, "what about the joking, the joshing, the poking fun?" Because we, the people who make cards, don't just talk about aging, we do something about it. Something funny.

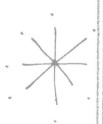

Middle-Aged Chopper

And this one has extra lumbar support, a bifocal windshield, and a built-in pill dispenser.

Cool.

And that land mass over there is called a "stick out" because of the way it sticks out into the water.

We got a letter from a woman saying this was the ONLY card she was going to send for the rest of her life.

inside:

ANotheR YeaR oldeR, anotheR YeaR closeR to Making uP CRAP.

Try listening to talk radio some very early Saturday morning and you'll actually hear stuff like this.

Hi! First-time caller! Let me say I agree with the last caller about bran. Bran rules! Prunes suck! Love your show...

TALK RADIO FOR PEOPLE YOUR AGE.

Many shoebox
staffers are
approaching the
"yelling at the
weatherman" age.

Daniels

You aren't officially old until you
start yelling at the weatherman.

Hazing rituals for people your age.

After writing several million birthday jokes, it gets harder to be objective about what's funny and what's JUST WEIRD. This card walks that fine line.

This is one of those cards that might seem dirty, but really isn't. Or _is_ it . . . ?
(Actually, no, it isn't. Sorry.)

THE BAD NEWS:

YOUR VISION GETS WORSE AS YOU GET OLDER.

inside:

THE GOOD NEWS:

YOU CAN'T SEE WHAT'S HAPPENING TO YOUR BODY.

The "Missing Glasses" Support Group

One of the artists loses her glasses at least once a day.

Don't even
act like
you haven't
done this.

BEFORE RUSHING into A FACE-LIFt,
Kim CHECKS OUt HOW iT LOOKS
On tHE CAT.

THE DWARVES AT 50

Touchy   Baldy   Squinty

Gassy   Chubby   Cranky   Drafty

Phoot

A-A-R-P! I WANNA JOiN THE A-A-R-P-!

THE RETIREMENT VILLAGE PEOPLE

Due to an apparent clerical error, the artist of this card has been on the AARP mailing list since he was about 12.

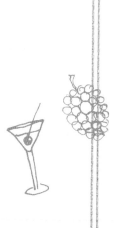

When 50-year-olds golf

Might be based on you if you were dining in a popular restaurant chain on May 8th, 1992. It became a card immediately. So, thank you.

Maxine Talks aBout AGiNG

* At my age, checks are the only things I've got that bounce.

* A little wine is good for your heart. And a great big whine is good for your attitude.

* Welcome to the years where just haulin' your butt around counts as a workout.

* I may be old, but people who look like me always win the lotto.

* At my age, the number one fashion question is: Can you nap in it?

* Life is an open road. Fortunately, at our age, we have lots of gas.

* At my age, caffeine has officially replaced ambition.

* Age is just a state of mind. If you state my age, I mind.

* Here's a makeup tip for women your age: Let the second coat dry thoroughly before applying the third.

* It's not menopause. I'm just like this.

It ONLY HURTS when I Laugh

Doctors are funny. Nurses are funny.
Hospital gowns? Comedy gold! It's almost
too bad the average Shoebox fan is so darn
healthy because, man, can we make fun of
it when they're not! You'll probably want
to take our word on this. Read two of these
and call us in the morning.

Humor aids in the healing process. Hence, the ~~great~~ *popularity* of this card.

inside:

They delivered your suppository.

If I were you, I'd get well real soon.

Are you sure you want to fix your trick knee? This is pretty cool.

When old guys dream.

Originally written about glazed donuts, but cheese fries had a better ring to it.

Anita

inside:

Obviously, there are some things insurance won't cover.

To the beloved hospital gown—
WE SALUTE YOU!

Larry's plan to completely cover his butt by wearing the hospital gown backward proves to have <u>one tiny flaw</u>.

A staff
favorite.
Well, among
the married
women
anyway.

Surgeons to Avoid

The TV show "Scrubs" is a favorite among the writers.

JUST ANOTHER DAY AT MEDICAL SCHOOL

9 out of 10

DOCTORS WANT you to Get Well immediately!

ebner

 The writer of this card can't even look at it because of his fear of needles.

inside:

THAT 10TH ONE THINKS YOU MIGHT STILL HAVE A COUPLE OF bucks SOMEWHERE.

I have this empty feeling inside.

REVILO

Hey, look! It's a theme!

I FEEL LIKE EVERYONE WANTS A PIECE OF ME.

STAN

Not surprisingly, this artist is a mother of <u>three</u>.

Does it concern anyone else out there that this card consistently rates high as a Father's Day Card? C'mon Dads. Get a new joke.

What's he Saying?

(Choose Your Favorite Message)

* So that's the story of how I
met your Grandmother and became
a man. Any questions?

* Yep. They really did used to take
your temperature there.

* ...And that Jimmy, is the tale
of my very first colonoscopy. ⟵

We come up
with different
ideas for
each card.
This is the
one we used.

* When I was your age, I'd already had
seven children, two mortgages, and
lost most of the feeling in my right
arm. It was a simpler time.

SigN of the TiMes

Lots of people can make a joke if you give them enough time. But making a joke out of something that just happened takes a different skill altogether. Or maybe the same skill, only faster. Something's different, but we're not sure what. We're a card company, not a think tank, so read these quickly or they won't be funny. Well, they might be a little funny, but not as funny as they would have been if you'd gotten busy and read them when we said. Slacker.

Note: Some Shoebox writers have been here long enough to remember when we couldn't put "sucks" on a card. Also when we had to walk to work uphill in the snow.

If that wasn't a thong, it is NOW.

Why they call it the "South Beach" diet.

TOP SIRLOIN PROTEIN BAR

ALL-MEAT SNACKS for the ATKINS DIET

MEATBALLS

FREEZER DOGS

LUNCHEON MEAT BOXES 6 PACK

MEAT ROLL-UPS

The High Protein/low-carb Craze proved to be a little too easy to mock.

The oldest living animal is the giant turtle, which eats no meat. <u>Chew on that.</u>

Make a wish and blow out YOUR birthday steak!

It's a new low-carb tradition.

MAD COWS

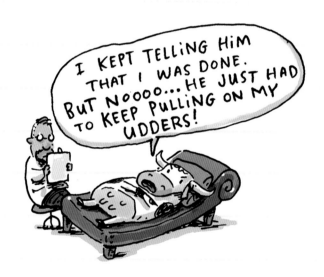

TRACEY begins to wonder if she's supporting too many causes.

Only a slight exaggeration of "support bracelets" worn by the writer's son.

Why Ally McBeal is single.

Maybe the hardest part of working at Shoebox is having to keep up with all the TV shows & movies.

whew.

There were several cards we decided not to include here because they were just too dated. Just like these will be in:

3, 2, 1...

CATS AWAY

...but what if everyone <u>does</u> Wang Chung tonight? Who's gonna look after the herd then?

← Big question over whether people would get this. They did, fortunately.

Good for people!

Hooray for baffling new technology & transportation! Without them, lots of cards wouldn't exist.

This card was inspired by the 2004 presidential race and is brilliantly non-partisan.

← Some guy liked this card enough to enter an in-house costume contest dressed as the character.

Congratulations on your promotion.
I'm sure you earned it.

A Hard Day's Laugh

We work very hard each day at our jobs.
For about 15 minutes. After that, it's
phone calls, e-mails, magazines, seeing if
anyone left anything unmarked in the
refrigerator, and one time, somebody got a
motorcycle and we took pictures of ourselves
sitting on it. But seriously, part of our
work is making cards about work. This is
the kind of thing that, if you really start
thinking about it, can freak you out and
you have to go get some coffee or maybe
just ride the elevator for a while.

This card
was actually
written on a
TUESDAY, but
the feeling
was the same.

brace

At 3:42 on a ThuRsday afternOon,

Ken reaLiZed tHat woRk

reaLLy dOes "suCk."

THE DAY THE SECRETARY STAYED HOME

We make fun of bosses, but in private, we *really* make fun of bosses.

1802 – JOHANN DECIMAL INVENTS THE POINT.

Font on decimal point is Helvetica **Bold.**

Your birthday calls for a group hug*.

*There has never been a group hug in Shoebox.

Interpretive dances, yes. But group hugs, no.

inside:
*The aforementioned hug (hereafter referred to as "the hug") is strictly metaphorical in nature. No actual hugging is implied or suggested or even recommended. If you (the birthday person) choose to hug yourself, we cannot/will not stop you, but all such hugging (of self) must be restricted to designated self-hugging approved zones (see map Attach A) and conducted in compliance with current (or future) hug guidelines (Attach B).

OFFICE PARTIES IN HELL

One of the
Shoebox artists
looks so young
she is often
smiled at and
given a cookie
on "Bring your
daughter to
work" day.

Bring-Your-Mom-
To-Work Day.

A frighteningly accurate depiction of our booths, except that they are cluttered with collectible action figures.

Butts at the office? GREETING CARD GOLD, BABY!

Top Ten Signs You're Stressed at work

Little things that people say to you every day suddenly seem irritating.

10. You are asked to stop using power tools at
    your desk, but it's just your teeth grinding.

9. You're drinking coffee directly from
   the pot, through a straw, while it's
   still brewing.

8. When a co-worker says, "Hello."
   You respond, "Eat toner and die!"

7. After you sharpen a brand new pencil,
   it's an inch and a half long.

6. You brought an axe to work to dislodge
   the cookies in the vending machine.

5. You won't stop calling the elevator
   an "oversized coffin."

4. You've named your computer "mouse."

3. You begin every e-mail you write
   with "Attention Fellow Losers."

2. Your office has lots of randomly
   hung art to cover up the holes
   you've punched in the walls.

1. You tell the boss to go outsource himself.

Relatively Funny

We all have family. We refer to them as "the rich soil in which to sow the seeds of humor and then harvest a bounty of jokes." Unless we're in a hurry, then we also call them "family." If you'd like to meet each and every member of yours, just win the lottery. They'll come out of the woodwork! Then you can ask them what they were doing in your woodwork.

Note: Loosely based on a real-life experience of an artist who shall remain unnamed.

Sisters never forget. This is both _good_ and _bad._

inside:

**With love to my sister,
my very first
and very best shrink.**

Based on an _actual_ sisterly relationship between the writer and her horrible sister.

When you go into the bathroom and you sit down on a seat that's already warm and it doesn't creep you out, well, that's family.

Ever noticed how in every family there's usually one person who's shockingly normal?

from the shameless self-promotion files:
Hallmark makes cards for over 100 different types of family relationships.

inside:

We should get ourselves one of those.

HOW PARENTS SEE THEMSELVES.

HOW KIDS SEE THEIR PARENTS!

"The first half of our lives is ruined by our parents, and the second half by children."

— Clarence Darrow

Mixing "age," "season," and "relatives" is tricky, but it works here.

Written by an
artist who enjoyed
two pregnancies
using this
very tactic.

A fine
example of
the rare,
one-word
cartoon

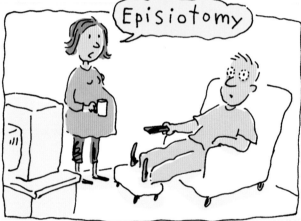

Renée

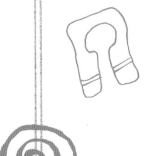

Ignored her mother's advice.

I do... What?

Weddings and Anniversaries are beautiful times. Beautiful for people who make jokes for a living. We cry, and our tears are tears of joy. We are also big fans of the little mints that you can only get at weddings. Mints of joy. If you would like to do the Chicken Dance as you read these, we won't stop you.

Note: More than one happy marriage owes its existence to another TV somewhere else in the house.

The bride + groom
cake topper look
suspiciously like
the artist and
her husband.

Words to Avoid
If You Write
Your Own Vows:

Bodacious
Foxy
Undulating
Whatever
Salami
Bargain
Litigation

Renée

Grab all the
happiness you can!

175

WALLY MISUNDERSTANDS THE CONCEPT OF TYING CANS TO THE BRIDE AND GROOM'S CAR.

"Marriage is a
great institution,
but I'm not
ready for an
institution yet."

— Mae West

TOILET HUMOR
WITH REAL
TOILETS!
Quality, cutting-
edge humor.

Trapeze-artist marriages have a level of communication that most do not enjoy.

AS THE YEARS PASSED BY, HERB AND EDNA GREW TO LOOK MORE AND MORE ALIKE.

This card was done by the late, great Bill Bridgeman, a longtime shoebox writer.

Note the
EXCELLENT
PLACEMENT
of the teddy's
ears!

On their anniversary,
Karen greeted David at
the door wearing nothing
but a teddy.

inside:

AN ANNIVERSARY TiP:
STAY iN, ORDER OUT.

Based on a
waiter at an
Italian chain
restaurant
who had
aspirations
of being
a comedian.
He's still
waiting tables.

for A SUCCESSFUL Marriage...

Do: Listen to each other and try not to smirk.

Don't: Try to use the remote to mute your spouse.

Do: Spoon in bed together.

Don't: Fork in a public place.

Do: Practice patience and understanding with your spouse.

Don't: Practice voodoo on your spouse.

R.P.K.

Do: Celebrate birthdays
and anniversaries.

Don't: Celebrate arguments
you've won by shouting
"In your face!"

Do: Take up a hobby
together.

Don't: Take up hatchet
throwing together.

Do: Kiss each other
good night.

Don't: Go to bed angry.
Or in spurs, which
can really rip up
a mattress.

Adults ONLY
SEXtion

Sex is funnier than you think. Unless you
already think it's funny, then you are
right up our alley, so to speak. This is
one of those areas where the "corporate
sensors" and the urge to be really funny
fight. It's a slow-motion fight where
a sprinkler unexpectedly goes off and they
both get their shirts wet and then they
well, you get the picture. Or you can
if you have a computer.

Written after a crazy night at a bachelorette party. While the card is funny, the party is still more memorable...

inside:

A girl can dream...

Is it just a 📐 coincidence that the author of this card has one AMAZING yard?

Make it sparkle, Mister!

Yes, my lady.

Walter found out too late that Helen's secret fantasy had nothing to do with sex.

This card wouldn't have worked had the genders been reversed. As funny as Men's secret fantasies may be, they're almost entirely inappropriate to print.

What is it with the elderly and sex, anyway? Actually, don't tell me. Please <u>do</u> <u>not</u> <u>tell</u> <u>me</u>.

As you grow older, remember -- you can still have the body of a 21-year-old.

This card was written long before Demi Moore made it fashionable to date younger men. Long before.

inside:

First, buy him a couple of drinks...

The writer of this card once threw out her back while typing (let alone anything else...)

At our age, kinky sex
takes on a whole new meaning.

"Is it not
strange that
desire should
so many years
outlive
performance?"

– William Shakespeare
Henry IV, part 2

The editor was
EMBARRASSED
when she finally
got the joke.

I HEAR THAT A WOMAN IN TULSA WAS TAKEN ABOARD AN ALIEN SPACECRAFT AND SUBJECTED TO ALL KINDS OF BIZARRE SEXUAL EXPERIMENTS.

inside:

YOU UP FOR A TRIP TO TULSA?

We've actually received letters asking us to stop making fun of aliens. You should see the return addresses...

WHEN POSSUM WIVES
AREN'T IN THE MOOD

Outings to
the Zoo aren't
just fun and
educational,
they're rife
with card
material!

The artist who
turned in this idea
actually owns a bird.
Coincidence?

Andy explains the universal sign
for "No refunds."

ConTROVeRSially SpeAKing..#.%&

You probably think that in the potpourri-
scented, pastel-hued world of greeting card
creation, nothing controversial can happen.
Well, you're wrong. It's more coffee-
scented. And, there's controversy. A sense
of humor is a subjective, personal,
capricious, and volatile thing. You learn
this quickly when you make fun of people
who don't know what capricious and volatile
mean. We believe that if we're not
offending somebody, then no one will be
offended. And where's the fun in that?

Note: He's not doing what you think
he's doing. Shame on you.

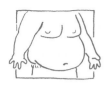

This ended up
being one of the
BEST-SELLING
shoebox cards, ever.

The masses
have spoken!
They love visors.

Oddly enough, the group we angered with this card was the labor union of a self-assembly furniture company.

THE NATIONAL COALITION OF FREE MEN

John G. Macchietto, Ph.D., 712 Prairie Wind, Stephenville, Texas 76401 • (817) 968-7582

March 16, 1991

Rene Hershey
Public Relations Director
Hallmark Cards, Inc.
McGee Trafficway
Kansas City, Missouri   64141

Dear Ms. Hershey,

I have enclosed a copy of my editorial in *Transitions* which is presently in press and will be distributed nationally soon. Your company's attitude and actions have bought you this coverage. I intend to continue bringing your company's male-bashing arrogance under public scrutiny.

If your position changes, I would be glad to publicize your new policy towards men in *Transitions*. Personally, I think your present position is not only degrading but very foolish.

Sincerely,

John G. Macchietto

John G. Macchietto, Ph.D.

JGM

Men
are
scum.

inside:

Excuse me. For a
second there, I was
feeling generous.

⇐ Written by
a man who
could make
a joke and
take a joke.

CSI: TOPEKA

"Looks like he was bored to death."

gordon.

"Why would you die of boredom when there's so much to do in Topeka? Besides, if you really want to be entertained we have the state legislature here."

— Topeka Mayor Bill Bunten (according to the Kansas City Star)

"...we try to acquire objects that speak to contemporary issues, some of them serious, some of them not so serious. Often they deal with the image of Kansas, good or bad....we would love to have a copy of the card for our collections..."

— Blair Tarr, Museum Curator, Kansas State Historical Society

And More from Mayor Bunten...

"I find it offensive. It's probably drawn up by somebody from West Virginia who hasn't been here."
(As seen in Newsweek)

Perhaps the most talked about card of 2005. Created a short-lived media frenzy.

RaNdom Acts of FuNNy

Humor, by its very nature, is rebellious. It doesn't fit into your labels and boxes, man. It wants to be free! Not literally, but, you know, figuratively. But seriously, categorizing jokes is tedious, time-consuming work. So we quit after a while and just put these here.

"HE HAD 13 ITEMS."

The grocery store is PROOF that we are not as civilized a country as we like to think.

JIM PAYS THE PRICE FOR WRITING AN EXTREMELY PERSONAL CHECK.

This really happened.

THINGS THAT ARE VAGUELY SCARY:

The coffee cup is a salute to the many instant drink machines around Hallmark that dispense FREE, yet SCARY, brown liquids.

wigs

taxidermy

public restrooms

instant coffee

adults with stuffed animals in their cars

smith

Sleep deprivation techniques are often used on the writers to induce hallucinations and VOILA, brilliant cards.

The artist used his second grade sketchbook for reference.

Maurice's first day as a courtroom sketch artist was also his last.

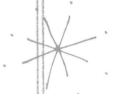

Less funny lines we didn't print:

- And I collect garden gnomes

- And I still live with my mom.

- And I scream like a girl.

The writer actually worked at a lemonade stand in his neighbor's driveway.

When life hands you lemons, make lemonade.

Anita

inside:

But when life hands you a load of crap, don't make anything.

Trust me on this one.

HOW TO TELL

IF YOU HAVE THE
RARE AND COVETED

"THIRD EYE":

STAND IN FRONT OF
A MIRROR AND SHUT
BOTH YOUR EYES.

IF YOU CAN STILL
SEE YOURSELF,
YOU HAVE
A THIRD EYE.

After this idea was turned in, it was recommended that the writer take a few days off to "regroup." It didn't help.

The fat pay raise this artist received was the result of brainwashing her manager with a similar technique.

We were out last week, trying to decide what to get you for graduation, when we drove by BILL'S. You remember BILL--he won all that MONEY in the lottery. He lives right by that GREEN field with the singing cows, the ones that keep going MOO-LA, MOO-LA. Anyway, as we drove to the CASH machine, we saw a deer by the side of the road-- I think it was a BUCK. THAT'S when I had a GRAND idea...

inside:

Ice cream! We should stop and get some ice cream!

So we did.

(Oh, yeah... and here's some money for you.)

If I gave you $10,000 for your birthday, what would you clear, like $7,000? Well, the government's not getting my three thousand, I'll tell you that right now!

stan

inside:

Happy Birthday
(Blame the government.)

A shoebox staffer once won $12,000 in the lottery and didn't even bring in donuts.

One of the
early Shoebox
artists rarely
wore a bra.
He _really_
should have.

Igor possessed few other skills, but he was a master of head games.

Note the perspective. Art school pays off!

Even more
unbelievable
than an elf,
a reindeer,
+ a snowman
playing football,
is the fact
that they
won the
state title
last year.

Much to Paddy's chagrin, it turned out to be a pot of **MOLD** at the end of the rainbow.

Maybe the only Shoebox card to use the word "chagrin."

funny, But NO

For every card that ends up in a store, there are many, many — let's throw in one more — many that don't make it. Why? Lots of reasons. Some are obvious, some are trade secrets that we can't tell you so quit asking. Read these and see if you can tell why they never made it to a store. Some cards are good for laughing, not so good for sending.

Another year older and you're still totally with it.

So am I, but in my case, the "it" is my husband.

FUNNY, but NO.

Happy Birthday from the perfect pair.

And my husband. (What can I say? They really are good.)

FUNNY, but NO.

shoebox lore:
Only about 20% of what a writer turns in gets accepted. Here, we ~~proudly~~ feature the other 80%.

She looked at him with a look that seemed to say, "I'm looking at you like this because I want to have sex with you."

FUNNY, but NO.

Europe, in a Nutshell:

PROS

Rich history + culture

CONS

Fat guys in speedos

CHRISTMAS JUST WOULDN'T BE THE SAME WITHOUT PEANUT BRITTLE.

OR JESUS.

FUNNY, but NO.

It's a drag to find out your card is "funny, but no." But what really sucks is when your card is just "No."

Honey, I wanted to surprise you on Valentine's day.

So I'm leaving you.

Bye

You're like the NBA of the 1980s.

You, too, have a Magic Johnson.

FUNNY, but NO.

I know there's like real problems in the world, big problems, but my cat peed on my yoga mat and I'm bummed.

Hi

FBN **FUNNY, but NO.** DAS

Happy Birthday, Son

FUNNY, but NO.

Don't leave this in the floor of your car, you slob.

Love you.

THE PERSON WHO FIRST SAID, "LIVE LIFE TO THE FULLEST" IS DEAD NOW, WHICH KIND OF MAKES ME LAUGH.

FBN

AJ

You're not too old to learn a new trick!

(ns.) Is "smell better" a trick?

H.B.D.

FUNNY, but NO.

IF THE ENGAGEMENT RING IS BIG ENOUGH, IT'S LIKE YOU'RE WEARING IT ON YOUR MIDDLE FINGER.

Honey, this Afghan your Mom gave us is really warm!

You trigger
a kind of
protective impulse.
I want to shield
you from the
dangers of
our world.

FUNNY, but NO.

EXCEPT
for birds that
fly right at
your head. How
creepy are they,
with their beaks
and talons and
the squawking?
you're on your
own if it's birds.
H.B.D.

IVE BEEN WAITING
A LONG TIME FOR
SOMEONE LIKE YOU.
HOW LONG?

FUNNY, but NO.

THEY SAY THAT THERE'S
A SOUTH AMERICAN
TICK THAT WILL WAIT
PATIENTLY ON A TREE
LIMB FOR OVER 3
YEARS ~~just~~ TO DROP
ON THE BACK OF ~~the~~
JUST THE RIGHT
WARTHOG.

THAT TICK IS NOTHING.
I SPIT ON THAT TICK.   13

SO YOU'RE GETTING
A LITTLE OLDER,
TRY GOING PLACES
YOU'VE NEVER
BEEN BEFORE

FUNNY, but NO.

You KNOW,
ACT LIKE YOUR
HAIR.

HB   AJ

when someone tells me "Into each life some rain must fall!" I like to dump a bucket of water on their head and say "You mean, kind of like that?!!"

FUNNY, but NO.

Dear Santa Claus, This is Billy. I wanted the RED PowerBot, not the BLUE one!!! Next time, get it right, stupid!

Love, Billy

I planned to get you heirloom jewelry for your birthday.

But Grandma rallied. Stupid modern medicine.

FUNNY, but NO.

Although none of these could ever be cards, they make their way onto a department bulletin board where they live on.

Sniff Sniff Sniff

FUNNY, but NO.

Lives with Mom
HUGEST SCI-FI FAN
Selfish Lover
NO SENSE OF HUMOR
UNPUBLISHED CARTOONIST
Lousy Tipper

FUNNY, but NO.

Thanks!
IF I WAS A
DOG, I'D LICK
YOUR FACE!

OH, WHAT THE
HECK... C'MERE!

Ewww!

Ick.

Gross!

It's your birthday, as the french say, ~~Laister~~ Laissez le Bon Temp Rouler!" or as we say, "Let the Good Times Roll!"

Hey, ours sounds better! For once ours sounds better! We win! U.S.A. U.S.A. Happy Bir+hday P.S. U.S.A.!

When you throw up, you find out that you're not really chewing up your food that well.

Try to keep your cake down.

Congrats on your pregnancy!

I pee'd on a stick once. I was in the woods. The results weren't positive.

Hey! Need somebody to kind of hit on your fiancé so you can see how he responds? 'Cause I totally will, if you like. I've got an outfit picked out.

Here's a fun game — Next time you get pulled over and the cop asks, "Do you know why I stopped you?" just start listing stuff.

The body in the trunk? The Uzzi? My meth lab?

AJ

According to countless panda stories, they RARELY mate.

Have a better birthday than a panda!

FUNNY, but NO.

It's the Get Well Monkey!

Get Well, more evolved creature!

Sorry, but I heard ~~~~~~~~ desperate measures are needed.

FUNNY, but NO.

Are you going to have a real birthday party or one of those fake "parties" where you try to sell me something?

I'll come either way. I'm just asking.

Is that the only thing you think about?

FUNNY, but NO.

The Gingerbread Plumber.

Another good thing
about small towns:
Kind'a chunky girls
can win the beauty
pageant.

Have a small town
beautiful birthday,

FUNNY, but NO.

For more funny,
but no's, go to
www.shoebox.com
where we occasionally
remember to update
the site with
new ones.

— Oh, look! Timmy's growing his third ball!

May the
holiday
wonders
never
cease.

FUNNY, but NO.

I confused my
library card with
my sub sandwich
card and read
10 books for
nothing.

Stupid Jared.

A
Shoebox
Artist's
Work Week
—

monday:

Tuesday:

Wednesday:

Thursday:

Thursday Night:

Friday Morning:

friday afternoon:

© HMK CDS

Blame This Book On...

Maura Cluthe

An impressive collection of striped socks, funky watches, and old pop bottles are just a few things that make Maura über-cool. Or maybe it's her fascination with vintage robots, or the way she can transform a bunch of squares into an energetic piece of art, (as proof, check out the cover of this book). When she isn't talking about Apples (the computers, not the fruit) with her fiancé, she might be doting on her two dogs and drinking bubble tea. Someone who just generally adds color wherever she goes, Maura (or Ra Ra if she happens to be your aunt), writes work e-mails that are full of exclamation points and smiley faces, which makes them a lot like Maura.

Mary K. Eakin

Mary Eakin is especially fond of chai tea, animals so ugly they're cute, cyber-bowling, fuzzy socks, and the word pickles. Some of these idiosyncrasies are, no doubt, due to the jarring coast-to-coast changes in her life. From the berry farm in rural Oregon where she was raised, she moved to San Francisco to study design, and, completing that, to Boston, where she joined a design firm. Mary is now a resident of Kansas City, far from any coast, and an employee of Hallmark Cards, where, among other things, she made a big contribution to designing this book.

Dan J. Taylor

Shoebox hit the humor jackpot when they hired a young kid from outside Chicago with no formal joke-writing experience. Twenty years later, that kid still writes jokes every day and is living proof that a man can channel a woman's thoughts and that a sense of humor keeps you young. Known for his freakishly fast ability to translate clever thoughts onto paper, those who are able to decipher his chicken-scratch penmanship won't regret the effort. Dan did most of the extra writing in this book, in addition to many of the cards featured. A proud husband, father, and fan of kung-fu movies, cigars, and cultural studies, this bio would've been a lot funnier if he'd written it himself.

Sarah B. Tobaben

If you are a very lucky writer, you get to have your work edited by Sarah Tobaben. Enthusiastic, encouraging, insightful, optimistic, positive, these are all words we use to describe Sarah, along with well-traveled and neo-groovy (which we made up just for her). Sarah has walked on the Great Wall of China and climbed up the great Kilimanjaro of Africa, so she was more than prepared to face the rigors of helping to create this book. We couldn't have done it without her efforts, which she tirelessly employed using all those traits from the second sentence. We know you'd want her to come work with you, but you can't have her, so forget it.

Renée C. Andriani

In answer to the question, "How, oh, how could a Shoebox card be any funnier?" we have Renée Andriani. Renée has the unique perspective of a wife, mother, pet lover, and a wildly curly haired Connecticut "dahhhhling" with the mouth of a longshoreman. She understands the tragedy of a red juice box squirted on to a white couch and can illustrate the accident including every piece of furniture and home décor that anyone has ever owned. Renée is a renaissance woman who did the flip cartoon in this book and thinks people who visit the Renaissance Fair in costume are #*%! idiots.

Shoebox

(Current Staff)

Signatures include: Cecilia Gonzalez, Julie Phipps, Anita (Colman), Maura Cushe, Ann Schleihs, Barbara Wiederholt, Tom Schluter, Marn Jensen, Karen Sullivan, Terry Runyan, Maureen Youren, Cathi Bolander, Lieane, JWagner, Barbu Loesing, Jackie Mallory, Sherry Hibler, Allyson Jones, Sarah Tobaben, Robyn Fabsits, Gordon, Burguay, Maria, John R Smith, Hella Song, Russ Ediger, Julie McFarland, Khanh Tu Pham, Kahern, Iz Gilstrap, Meg Cundiff, Stan Makowski, Renée Andriani, Dan Woodall, Barbara C. Edgerton, Dick Daniels

Karen Porterfield • Kevin Ahern • Renée Andriani • Vince Andriani • Lainie Bassett • Dawn Braet • Eric
Julie McFarland • Marn Jensen • Liz Gilstrap • Sherri Shepherd • Sarah Tobaben • Maura Cluthe • Ann Sc
Schleihs • Maureen Gowen • Karen Porterfield • Kevin Ahern • Renée Andriani • Vince Andriani • Lainie Ba
Bassett • Dawn Braet • Eric Brace • Oliver Christianson • Denise Chevalier • Anita Colman • Meg Cundiff •
• Dick Daniels • Kim Ebner • Robyn Fabsits-Grine • Brian Gordon • Chris Harding • Cathy Law-Wilkerson •
• Cathy Liesner • Barbi Loesing • Stan Makowski • Maria O'Keefe • Gary Pratt • John Smith • Hella So
Song • Karen Sullivan • John Wagner • Bill Wagoner • Steve Finken • Peter Martin • Russ Ediger • Lee F
Franklin • Bill Gray • Allyson Jones • Tina Neidlein • Deeann Stewart • Dan Taylor • Barb Edgerton •
• Jackie Mallory • Mike Overmyer • Binh Pham • Fred Taylor • Scott Brown • Kim Newton • Dan Woodall •
• Carol Grimm • Cecilia Gonzalez • Barb Wiederholt • Tom Schulze • Julie Phipps • Jem Sullivan • Jana Br
Brunner • Patty Manners • Lottie Chestnut • Roxie Jerde • John Beeder • Greg Raymond • Homer Evans •
• Joy Bohannon Weaver • Debbie Dibal • Debbie Brown • Sarah Enger • Jeff Wilson • Andy Newcom • Jeff We
Webber • Bonnie Haskew McMullen • Leslie Kemp • Ed Odell • Robin Younger • Jeanne Slater • Mary Alice C
Craig • Ellen Junger • Bob Brush • Lew Nickerson • Payton Kelly • Becky Wilson Kelly • Juli Koontz Al
• Alice Broughton • Cheryl Gaines • Becky Richmond • Kristin Duncan • Diana Stuart • Chris Brethwaite B
• Bob Lucas • Rich Warwick • Mr. Toasthead • Kristi Stanley • Myra Zirkle • The Sessionaires • Kevin
"Shy Guy" Kinzer • Cherish Pageau • Kristin Duncan • Harold Barnes • John Ball • Trish Davis • Dave
Johnson • Pam Snyder • Jim Wuthrich • Christie Wilson • Leslie Foster • Tim Bowers • Dave Ko
Kornfeld • Alan Denney • Scott Oppenheimer • Marita Favreau •
Karen Oatman • Mark Oatman • Don Batson • Renee Duvall • Rob So
Scott • Bill Bridgeman • Warren Ludwig • Terri Steiger • I
Don Batson • Dave Biegelson • Dana David • Teresa Jarzemkoski •
• Mike Willard • Val McKeown Coursen • Deb Munson • Karen Ta
Tarpenning • Lucy Ware • John Sullivan • Kathy Krzesinski •
Sandy Defoe • Mark Jones • Lisa Tallarico • Bob Holt • Jo
John Peterson • Anne Blumer • LeAnne Mebust • Jane Moses •
Wing Ngo • Karen Brunke • John Hunt • Lyla Bridges • Mark Co
Cordes • Margaret Perez Weakley • Carleen Powell •
Mike Takagi • Lisa Tallarico • Julie Kangas • Christina Ma
Maluccelli Vann • Lori Osecki Lizz Miller Pembroke • Jean Bo
Boehm • John Dill • Jennifer Plecas • Debby Glasgow • Mark Franzke • Carol Walz Sheldon •
• Cathi Bolander • Melissa Duff-Cohen • Charlie Henderson • Jim Bourgeois • Brett Bennett • Rachel Br
Britt • Shirley Manka • Annette Esler • Tony Frerking • Bev Rickman • Enrique Paz • Vince Yzon • Or
Orville Wilson • Kirk Lawther • Susan Pauli • Rinda Cooper • Reed Russell • Cyndi Hochstatter • Rowena
Young • Denny Steiner • Shelly Coppin • Joann Bergt • Mary Herera • Carl Moore • Zura Stewart • Terry O'
O'Reagan • Debbie Giglione • Deb Hernandez • Stephanie Hsiung • Sandi Sumada • Cheryl Smith • Jaqui Mo
Moore • Darrel Holtz • Betty Pitts • Eric Skubish • Terri Kneale • Teresa Messick • Stacey Johnson Do
Donovan • Kim Lee • Linda Monahan • Kathy Patton • Joyce Hulett • Kathy Reed • Dave Lykens • Marty
Heath • Tom Mulqueen • Anne Angotti • Jane Boone • Karen Mabry • LeAnne Coder • Cleon Braun • Linda Pl
Plattner • Scott Hobbs • Sally Caron • Jay Dahlberg • Randy Knipp • Maggie Weston • Kathy Dunaway • Ka
Karen McBee • Carol Wilbers • Ed Place • Dave Froelich • Curt Samson • Denee Meyer • Huong Doan • J
Lisa Robertson • Jill Bauer • Gary Jacobson • Laura Bolter • Cathy Rowe • Leeanne Mebust • Patty Gi
Gillis • Dave Biegelsen • Paul Quick • Christy Wilson • Sharon Van Orden • Rita Lewis • Kris Ma
Mangiaracina • Gail Ryther • Jenise Johnson-Carl • Brian Grubb • Mark Zolton • John Jennings • Cheryl V
Vanderford • Susan Bruna • Herb Dessinger • Joann Burt • Diana Turner • James Jorns • Sharon Thomas •
• Nancy Briggs • Mark Mattern • Bob Kolar • Scott Mack • Michelle Berg • John Foster • Steve Skelton •
• Danyse Skelton • Ed Wallerstein • Richard Bagley • Jim Howard • Aimee Doyen • Syd Baker • Colleen Le
Laughlin • Becky Rellihan • Ric Brockmeier • Cynthia Witte • Rhonda Driskell • Dan Walsh • Christine O
Overgaard • Theresa Steffens • Shelley Mathews • Julie McFarland • Marn Jensen • Liz Gilstrap • Sherri S
Shepherd • Sarah Tobaben • Maura Cluthe • Ann Schleihs • Julie McFarland • Marn Jensen • Liz Gilstrap

Shoebox wouldn't be Shoebox
without all the people who have
come and gone the past 20 years.
  Here's to everyone who has ever
helped make the thousands of
Shoebox card ideas a reality.
Our apologies to anyone we missed.
Don't be mad. Although you're
cute when you're mad.